DOCUMENTED BRIEFING

RAND

The Thrift Savings Plan

Will Reservists Participate?

Beth J. Asch, John T. Warner

Prepared for the
Office of the Secretary of Defense

National Defense Research Institute

PREFACE

The FY2000 National Defense Authorization Act provided authority to members of the armed services to participate in the federal thrift savings plan (TSP). The structure of the TSP for service members would be similar to the one that covers civil service personnel who participate in the Civil Service Retirement System. Members would be able to contribute up to 5 percent of their basic pay, but there would be no government contributions. The one difference from the TSP that covers civil service personnel is that military members would be able to contribute their special and incentive pays.

The Federal Thrift Retirement Investment Board conducted a cost analysis and concluded that extending TSP participation to members of the part-time Ready Reserve would be wasteful and a bad idea because the cost of administering a large number of small accounts would be extraordinarily high. The Board recommended that part-time reservists be excluded from participation.

The Office of the Secretary of Defense (Reserve Affairs and Compensation, jointly) requested that the analysts working as part of the 9th Quadrennial Review of Military Compensation (QRMC) study this issue. This briefing summarizes our analysis in response to that request. The analysis was conducted within a short time-frame and uses available data sources to estimate the number of part-time reserve participants and their annual expected account contribution. The briefing concludes by offering several policy options.

This research was conducted in part under the sponsorship of the Office of Special Studies, Office of the Under Secretary of Defense for Personnel and Readiness. It was also partly conducted under the sponsorship of the 9th Quadrennial Review of Military Compensation. It was performed within the Forces and Resource Policy Center of RAND's National Defense Research Institute, a federally funded research and development center sponsored by the Office of the Secretary of Defense, the Joint Staff, the unified commands, and the defense agencies.

CONTENTS

ACKNOWLEDGMENTS

We would like to thank several individuals for their contribution to this analysis. We thank John Enns and Curt Gilroy, director and co-director of the 9th Quadrennial Review of Military Compensation, for their support and comments. We also benefited from the input of Jim Hosek, Sue Hosek, and Stan Panis at RAND, and we appreciate the helpful comments of our RAND reviewer, Elaine Reardon. We wish to thank Stephanie Williamson and Scott Naftel at RAND and Michael Dove and Tim Elig at the Defense Manpower Data Center for helping us access and create analysis files from the Reserve (RCCPDS) Master Files and the 1992 Reserve Enlisted and Officer Surveys. We would also like to thank Captain Lou Farrell and Virginia Hyland in OSD (Reserve Affairs), Chuck Wischonke in OSD (Compensation), and Michael Hansen at the Center for Naval Analyses for their input. Finally, we benefited from the comments we received from the working group members of the 9th Quadrennial Review of Military Compensation.

The FY2000 National Defense Authorization Act provides the authority for members of the uniformed services to participate in the federal TSP. The structure of the TSP for service members would be similar to the structure of the TSP that covers those personnel in the federal civil service who participate in the Civil Service Retirement System (CSRS). Members could contribute up to 5 percent of their basic pay. Unlike participants in CSRS, those in the armed forces could contribute their special and incentive pays as well. However, the maximum annual contribution is $10,500. As with the CSRS participants, the members' contributions would not be matched by the government.

There are two main obstacles to implementing the TSP for members of the uniformed services. The first obstacle involves finding the funds to cover the cost of covering military personnel. A qualifying offset must be found to fund this program. This obstacle is not addressed in our analysis.

The other primary obstacle is that the Federal Thrift Retirement Investment Board, which we call the TSP Board, opposes the participation of part-time ready reservists in the TSP because the cost of administering their accounts would be prohibitively high. According to their calculations (Roger Mehle, letter to Rudy deLeon, December 1999), participation by part-time ready reservists would involve many accounts that would be small in terms of their annual dollar contributions. Since it would not be fair to burden the federal civil service members with this cost, the cost would have to be borne by military personnel. The board estimates that the administrative costs associated with managing so many small accounts would require a 8.4 percent charge on the part-time reservists' account balances.

The administrative cost is based on the number of accounts and their average size. The board estimates that the number of accounts would be 132,000, equal to the number of eligible part-time ready reservists (825,000) times a participation rate of 16 percent. The 16 percent figure is based on the observed annual TSP contribution rate of CSRS participants; that rate is 20 percent. To account for the lower (or "service") earnings of the reserve population, the TSP Board normalized the rate for part-time reservists to 16 percent.

The board also estimates that the average annual contribution of a part-time reservist would be just above $200. Roughly, this figure is based on average reserve basic pay ($4892) times an assumed annual contribution rate of 4.2 percent.

The TSP Board's estimate of the reserve participation rate—16 percent—may be too high, for two main reasons.

First, part-time reservists are civilians, and many of them work for employers that not only already offer a retirement plan like the TSP but whose plans provide an employer match to the employee's contributions. That is, those plans are better in terms of their expected benefit levels than the TSP. For those reservists, the TSP would not be an improvement over what they could get in their civilian jobs.

Second, some reservists have characteristics that are not associated with participation in retirement plans. For example, they are more likely to be young males. This could cause the participation rate to be lower than what the TSP Board estimates.

This chart shows conceptually which reservists might be made better off by the reserve TSP option and which are no worse off. The left-hand column lists the various types of retirement plans available to part-time reservists in the civilian sector. The right-hand column indicates whether the reserve TSP option is an improvement over each type of civilian retirement plan.

The first type of retirement plan is known as a defined contribution (DC) plan. The TSP belongs to this class of plans. Under a DC plan, contributions are made to a fund and the individual has various choices for how that fund is invested. The value of one's retirement benefit depends on the level and pattern of contributions and on the fund's performance over time. DC plans have become quite pervasive in the civilian labor market. Under some DC plans, the employers match the employee contributions; under others, they do not. Clearly, the reserve TSP is less attractive than a civilian plan where the employer matches the worker's contributions.

The other primary type of plan is a defined benefit (DB) plan. Under a DB plan, the retirement benefit is based on a formula. Many civilian employers cover workers with both a DB and a DC plan. The Federal Employees Retirement System (FERS) is an example of such a plan. Most state and local workers are covered by a DB plan only. Active-duty personnel are also only covered by a DB plan, the military retirement plan. The reserve TSP is an improvement over a DB plan only because it offers a retirement option that is not

5

available to them under their DB plan, an opportunity to put pre-tax dollars into an investment fund that can be rolled over to an individual retirement account (IRA) if the individual separates from the employer before he or she is eligible for retirement.

The final type of plan that covers part-time reservists is no plan. Those without a retirement plan can open an IRA that allows them to save pre-tax dollars in a retirement fund. Since the reserve TSP may offer the same opportunity, whether the reserve TSP is an improvement depends on a member's reserve earnings, civilian earnings, and marital status. The reserve TSP has a 5 percent cap on contributions from earnings. The IRA cap is $2000. If the reserve cap is binding such that members who want to contribute as much as $2000 cannot do so because their reserve earnings are too small, the IRA could be better. On the other hand, if the reserve cap is not binding and members want to contribute more than $2000, the reserve TSP is better because members can contribute up to $10,500. Also, whether IRA contributions can be tax-deferred depends on income level and marital status. Since all TSP contributions would be tax-deferred regardless of income and marital status, the TSP might be better for some individuals.

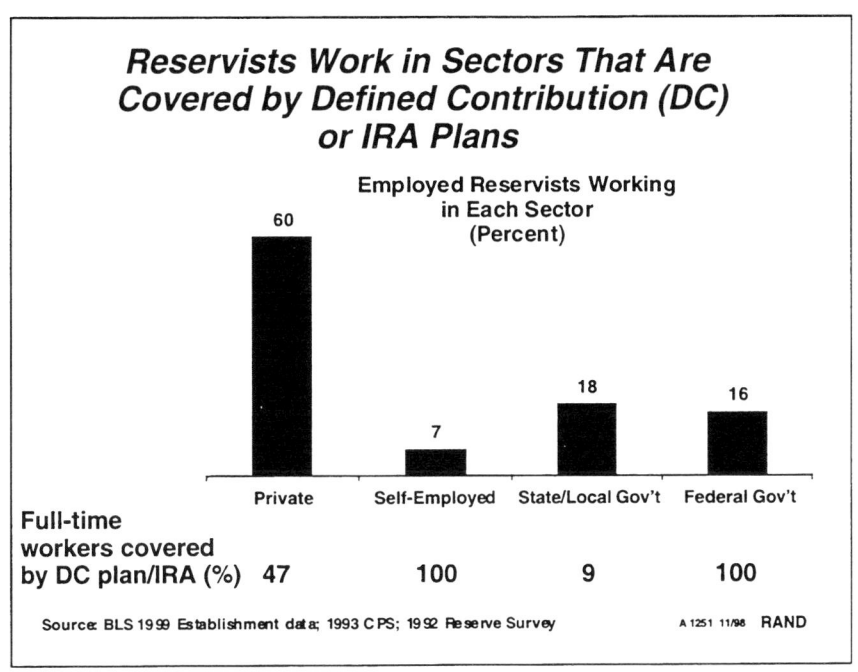

Reservists Work in Sectors That Are Covered by Defined Contribution (DC) or IRA Plans

Employed Reservists Working in Each Sector (Percent)

	Private	Self-Employed	State/Local Gov't	Federal Gov't
	60	7	18	16

| Full-time workers covered by DC plan/IRA (%) | 47 | 100 | 9 | 100 |

Source: BLS 1999 Establishment data; 1993 CPS; 1992 Reserve Survey

A 1251 11/98   RAND

The previous chart showed that part-time reservists who have DC plans, especially those that provide an employer match, are unlikely to be better off with a reserve TSP. This chart shows how part-time reservists are distributed across sectors, and what fraction of full-time workers in these sectors have DC plans. Because of the distribution of reservists across jobs covered by a DC plan, some reservists are likely to be covered by a DC plan and therefore, are not likely to view the reserve TSP option as an improvement.

Most part-time reservists work for private-sector employers. Almost half (47 percent) of full-time private sector workers are covered by a DC plan. A large proportion of reservists, larger than the civilian population as a whole, work for the federal government. Because the TSP is offered to all full-time civil service employees, even those participating in CSRS, 100 percent of full-time federal government employees are covered by a DC plan. Similarly, because all self-employed workers have the opportunity to open an IRA, all self-employed workers are covered by a DC plan. Only the state and local sector has few jobs covered by a DC plan. This sector usually only has a DB plan. About 20 percent of part-time reservists work in this sector.

While the TSP Board's estimate of the reserve participation rate might be too high, its estimate of the average account contribution might be too low. Account contributions might be higher because part-time reservists would be allowed to contribute their special and incentive pays, a factor not incorporated by the board's estimate of the average account balance. Also, if prior-service personnel were allowed to transfer their active account balances to their reserve accounts, the size of reserve account balances would obviously be higher. Furthermore, because military technicians are federal workers, they already maintain accounts associated with their federal employment. If personnel could consolidate their federal and reserve account balances, the average reserve account size would be larger. Whether it is feasible to permit consolidation of accounts is an open question and needs further investigation.

The objective of our analysis is to use available data sources to derive our own estimate of the part-time reserve participation rate and the average reserve account balance.

As we describe in the rest of briefing, we estimate the reserve participation rate in the TSP while attempting to control for several key factors. First, we attempt to control for whether the individual might already have a DC plan with his or her civilian employer and, therefore, have little incentive to participate in the reserve TSP. Second, we attempt to control for the extent to which reservists would have an incentive to participate in a nonmatching contribution plan; individuals might respond differently to the incentive to shelter income from taxes, the main economic incentive for having a nonmatching plan. Finally, we attempt to control for the characteristics of the reserve population and how they differ from the civilian population as a whole. These characteristics may make reservists more or less likely than the civilian population to participate in a TSP. The data are from the early 1990s and display occasional shortcomings in consistency and quality; we discuss these data issues later.

We also attempt to estimate the average reserve account contribution and try to include special and incentive pays where possible. Finally, we highlight some of the policy implications of our findings.

One of the factors we attempt to incorporate into the
analysis—whether an individual will participate in a nonmatching
plan—is difficult to estimate because of the quality of the data
available.

Two data sources are publicly available to address this issue: the
Bureau of Labor Statistics (BLS) establishment data, which surveys
employers about their retirement plans, and the Current Population
Survey (CPS) April 1993 Supplement, which surveys individuals in
the civilian population about their retirement plans. The BLS data
tend to overestimate the coverage of workers in nonmatching plans
because they query employers about the retirement plans for the
"eligible" workforce, and not the entire workforce. The eligible
workforce is usually smaller than the entire workforce, implying that
the coverage rate is higher.

In some instances, the BLS data indicate coverage rates for the entire
workforce. These published rates allow us to compare the rates
found in the BLS data with those found using the CPS data. The CPS
rates are invariably smaller. Some workers in the CPS appear to be
unsure about their own pension plan coverage. Since employers are
better informed about their retirement plans, the rates in the BLS
data are higher. (The appendix describes the discrepancy between
the BLS and CPS.) We use the CPS data to estimate the reserve
participation rate. To address the problem of under-reporting in the

10

CPS data, we weight the CPS data to produce the pension coverage rates reported by the BLS for the entire workforce.

To estimate the reserve participation rate in a nonmatching TSP, we use the fraction of CPS respondents who have an IRA in the civilian sector, adjusted for age and other characteristics of reservists. IRA coverage is a good proxy of TSP participation because, like the reserve TSP, IRA contributions are not matched by the employer.

Furthermore, like the TSP, contributions may be tax-exempt. However, unlike the TSP option, under some circumstances IRA contributions cannot be sheltered from taxation. Those who are already covered by an employer plan and who earn less than $35,000 (rising to $60,000 by the year 2008) can contribute tax-exempt dollars. However, those who earn more than these limits cannot. Because some workers cannot contribute tax-exempt dollars to an IRA while all reservists would be able to contribute tax-exempt dollars to the TSP, it is possible that the IRA coverage rate might underestimate the participation rate in a nonmatching TSP. As discussed later, we conduct sensitivity analyses and discover that even if the estimated rate were considerably higher than what we find, our general conclusions about the level of participation would largely be unchanged.

While using IRA coverage as a proxy of TSP participation has several advantages, one disadvantage is that some individuals who have an IRA do not contribute to it annually. Furthermore, some who have an IRA also have a matching DC plan with their employer. The CPS data do not provide reliable information on IRA contributions or DC plan coverage among those with an IRA. We attempt to address these problems by adjusting the IRA participation rate in the CPS by the probability of having a DC plan with one's employer.

This chart indicates in more detail how we estimate the part-time reserve TSP participation rate. The participation rate is assumed to be the product of two probabilities. The first is the probability that an individual is not already covered by a DC plan, and therefore has no reason to participate in the reserve TSP. The second is the probability that an individual would participate in a nonmatching plan to shelter some income from taxes. Both probabilities are relevant because some reservists who might want to shelter income from taxation will already have an incentive to do so with their civilian employer.

We compute these probabilities using the 1993 CPS April Supplement data on the civilian population. We estimated probit models for the probability that an individual will have a DC plan and the probability that he or she will have an IRA. The results provide estimates of how the probabilities would vary among individuals with different characteristics such as age, marital status, earnings, ethnicity, full-time work status, and employer size and type (private, federal, state, and local). The probability of not having a DC plan is set equal to 1 minus the probability of having a DC plan. The probability of participating in a nonmatching plan is estimated to be the probability of having an IRA. (The probit results are reported in the appendix.)

Note that we compute the probability of *having* an IRA, not the probability of *contributing* to it. About 25 percent of the civilian

12

population has an IRA, according to the Employee Benefits Research Institute (EBRI, 1999), but only 5 percent contributes to it. Ideally, we would like to compute the probability of contributing to an IRA rather than having an IRA, since the former measure more closely estimates the probability of contributing to a reserve TSP. Furthermore, if we could estimate the probability of contributing to an IRA, it would not be necessary to adjust it by multiplying it by the probability of having a DC plan, since those who contribute to an IRA would have already incorporated their DC plan coverage in their decision to contribute to an IRA. Unfortunately, the CPS data do not provide a reliable measure of IRA contributions; therefore, we compute the probability of having an IRA. Since some of those who have an IRA may also have a DC plan to which they contribute, we multiply this probability by the probability of having a DC plan, as described above.

Once we estimate the probit equations, we then apply the probit results from the CPS to a random sample of part-time (i.e., non-Active Guard and Reserve) ready reservists, provided by the 1992 reserve personnel survey. Specifically, we predict the probabilities for each reservist in the sample, multiply them, and take the mean value. The mean gives us an estimate of the average TSP participation rate adjusting for the characteristics of reservists.

This methodology embeds some key assumptions. First, it assumes that those already covered by a DC plan will not choose to participate in the reserve TSP. This assumption is probably safe, although a few individuals might participate in a reserve TSP despite their already being covered by a DC plan. Second, it assumes that the rate of participation in the TSP equals the rate of participation in an IRA for similar individuals. As discussed in the previous chart, not all IRA contributions may be tax-exempt, and we may underestimate TSP participation on this count. However, as discussed later, our general conclusions are not sensitive to variations in this rate.

Reservists Have Characteristics That Raise the Probability of Already Having a DC Plan

Characteristic	Effect on probability of having DC plan*	Reserve relative to civilian population**
Age	+	Lower
Earnings	+	Higher
Male	–	Higher
White	+	Lower
Married	+	Higher
Works for large private employer	+	Lower
Works full-time	+	Lower
Federal worker or self-employed	+	Much higher

* Source: April 1993 CPS data
** Source: April 1992 CPS data and 1992 reserve survey

A 1251 11/98 RAND

The probit results relating to how the probability of contributing to a DC plan varies with individual characteristics are shown in the middle column of this chart. These results are obtained using the CPS 1993 April Supplement data. The right-hand column indicates how the reserve sample differs from the civilian sample in terms of the mean values of the characteristic. A more detailed description of the probit results, and the means characteristics of the two samples, are provided in the appendix.

Age and earnings are both positively related to having a DC plan in the CPS data, as is size of employer. Those working for the federal government obviously are more likely to have a DC plan because all federal full-time workers are covered. Reservists differ from the general population in these characteristics; for example, they are younger. Since they tend to be better educated, they earn more than civilians do. Furthermore, because their earnings are higher on average, this characteristic makes them more likely than civilians to have a DC plan.

Reservists Are More Likely to Have a DC Plan than Civilian Employees

Mean predicted probability of:	Reservists	Civilians
Having DC plan	59.3%	20.0%
Not having DC plan	40.7%	80.0%

Probability that a reservist participates in TSP =

Probability of not already having a Defined Contribution (DC) plan in civilian job x Probability of participating in nonmatching TSP

A 1251 11/98   RAND

We apply the probit results to the 1992 reserve survey data and compute a predicted probability of having a DC plan, and of not having a DC plan, for each part-time reservist in the survey. We then compute the mean probability in the sample. This chart shows the results and compares them to the rates found in the CPS data for the civilian population. (As discussed earlier, the CPS data are weighted to produce the mean pension coverage rates found in the BLS data.)

We estimate that 59.3 percent of reservists would already have a DC plan with their civilian employer, based on their characteristics and based on how those characteristics map into plan coverage in the civilian population. Since 1 – 59.3 percent is 40.7 percent, we estimate that 40.7 percent of reservists do not already have a DC plan with their civilian employer. This figure is the first of the two probabilities that we need to compute.

Reservists Have Characteristics That Lower Probability of Having a Nonmatching IRA

Characteristic	Effect on probability of having an IRA*	Reserve relative to civilian population
Age	+	Lower
Earnings	+	Higher
Male	–	Higher
Black	–	Higher
Married	+	Higher
Works for large private employer	–	Lower
Works full-time	–	Lower

*Estimated from civilian data

A 1251 11/98   RAND

The second probability we need to compute is the probability that a part-time reservist would participate in a nonmatching TSP. The first step is to estimate a probit model of having an IRA plan using the CPS data. The middle column summarizes the estimated effect of each characteristic on the probability of having an IRA. The probit results are shown in the appendix. As the chart indicates, both age and earnings are positively associated with having an IRA in the CPS data, as is being married. The last column indicates how the reserve mean characteristic compares with the civilian population mean. Reservists have characteristics that both lower and raise the probability of having an IRA. For example, they are younger than the general population; those who are younger are less likely to have an IRA.

We use the probit results to predict the probability of having an IRA for each part-time reservist in the reserve survey. Taking the mean, we estimate that 20.7 percent of reservists would have an IRA. The same proportion of civilians—20.4 percent—also have an IRA. The 20.7 percent figure forms the basis of the second probability that we need to compute the reserve participation rate.

To compute the overall reserve participation rate, we predict the probability of not having a DC plan and the probability of having an IRA for each individual in the reserve personnel survey data, and we take the product of these probabilities for each individual. We then compute the mean of this product across all reservists.

We estimate that, overall, 6.8 percent of part-time reservists would participate in the reserve TSP option. We can compute the mean rate for different subgroups of reservists, such as by component. For example, given the age and other characteristics of Navy reservists and those in the Coast Guard reserve, individuals in these components are found to be more likely to participate than those in the Marine Corps reserve and Army National Guard. Similarly, officers and prior-service personnel are more likely to participate than enlisted personnel and nonprior-service personnel. Still, none of the rates that we predict for the various subgroups is large. Therefore, we predict that relatively few part-time reservists are likely to participate in a reserve TSP option.

To estimate the number of participants, we need to multiply the participation rate by the number of part-time ready reservists. Since the TSP Board's objections concerned only the accounts of those reservists who serve in the military part-time, we only need to include those reservists who drill part-time.

Although the reserve components consist of 1,271,000 reservists, only 871,000 are in the Selected Reserves. Of these, only 806,000 are part-time reservists who are not serving on active duty full-time. This 806,000 includes the 57,000 military technicians who are federal civil service employees who work for the reserve components. Since military technicians drill on a part-time basis, they are included in our count. However, because they are also civil service employees, and therefore already have a DC plan, they are excluded from our estimate of the number of participants (see the computation in next chart).

The figures in this chart are based on the FY99 reserve components inventory, provided by the Defense Manpower Data Center's Information Delivery Service.

```
┌─────────────────────────────────────────────────────────────────┐
│                                                                   │
│         Our Estimate of Reserve Participation Is Lower            │
│                  than That of the TSP Board                       │
│                                                                   │
│                                    QRMC       TSP Board           │
│                                                                   │
│   Estimated participation rate     6.8%         16%               │
│                                                                   │
│   Number of part-time                                             │
│     ready reservists              806,000*     825,000            │
│                                                                   │
│   Expected number of participants  54,800      132,000            │
│                                                                   │
│                                                                   │
│   If prior-service reservists can contribute to their active duty │
│   accounts, the estimated number of reserve accounts will be      │
│   even lower                                                      │
│                                                                   │
│                                                                   │
│   *Source: DMDC IDS; excludes AGR                                 │
│                                               A 1251 11/98  RAND   │
│                                                                   │
└─────────────────────────────────────────────────────────────────┘
```

Our 6.8 percent estimated reserve participation rate is less than the
TSP Board's 16 percent figure, and our figure of 806,000 part-time
reservists is less than the 825,000 figure used by the TSP Board.
Given these differences, we estimate fewer participants.

To estimate the number of part-time reserve participants, we apply
the 6.8 percent figure to the 806,000 part-time reservists figure. We
estimate the total number of participants to be 54,800, a figure that is
considerably smaller than the 132,000 participants estimated by the
TSP Board.

The estimated number of participants might be even smaller,
depending on what types of account transfers and account
contributions would be allowed. If prior-service reserve personnel
could contribute to accounts that they created while they were on
active duty, they would not need to contribute to a reserve account,
and the estimated number of reserve accounts would be even
smaller that what is estimated here. Estimating how much smaller is
beyond the scope of our analysis, because it would involve
estimating the participation rate and separation rate of active-duty
personnel as well as the reserve affiliation rate of active-duty
participants.

The next part of our analysis focuses on estimating the average
dollar amount that a part-time reservist would contribute annually,
given that he or she contributes at all. Because of uncertainty about
whether special and incentive pays should be treated differently
from basic pay, we use two alternative methods to make this
computation.

The first method assumes that reservists would contribute to their
TSP from their special and incentive pays at the same rate as they
would contribute from their basic pay. That is, we can simply
consider total reserve earnings and apply an assumed contribution
rate. If we use the same contribution rate as the one assumed by the
TSP Board—4.2 percent—the first method involves multiplying 4.2
percent with the reserve earnings of each member in the reserve
survey sample, and taking the average.

The second method assumes that reservists would contribute a
higher percent of their special and incentive pays than they would
contribute of their basic pay. Such might be the case if reservists
receive lump-sum bonuses for serving in the reserve components. If
their existing retirement plans only allow paycheck deductions and
preclude lump-sum payments to the plans, individuals may find it
easier and less costly to deposit their lump-sum bonus in a reserve
TSP. Since we have no data to compare at what rate individuals

might contribute a lump-sum payment versus the rate that they might contribute from their monthly pay, we assume that individuals contribute 100 percent of their bonus payments. While 100 percent is clearly too high, it provides us with an upper-bound estimate of what the average TSP contribution is likely to be under this computational method. Since not everyone in the reserves gets a bonus, and bonuses are usually paid in installments, we must compute the expected annual bonus for reservists. We do that as follows.

First, we randomly assign a bonus to 18 percent of enlisted reservists in the reserve survey. DMDC data on reserve personnel from FY98 indicate that 18 percent of enlisted personnel received incentive bonuses, and less than 1 percent of officers received a bonus that was not a health professional loan repayment.

Next, we must assume a dollar amount for the bonus payment. The reserve components offer an array of bonus types that include reserve enlistment bonuses, reenlistment bonuses, and reserve affiliation bonuses. These bonus types differ in both their maximum annual payment and in their pay-out schedule. Some bonuses are paid out over several years in annual lump-sum installments, while others, especially if the dollar amount is small, are paid in one year. Few bonus types pay more than the maximum of $2500 in a given year, and not all individuals are eligible to receive those that do.

Of those individuals awarded a bonus in the reserve sample, we assume that the annual bonus installment payment is $2500, regardless of bonus type. If anything, the $2500 figure is probably too large, given that few reservists are likely to be eligible for an installment payment that high. We chose this larger figure because we prefer to overestimate—rather than underestimate—the average contribution of a reserve TSP participant. As will be seen in the following charts, even when we choose to overestimate the average annual contribution, we find that the average is relatively small, as the TSP Board contends.

We then compute for each reservist the expected contribution, equal to (4.2 percent x basic pay) + (100 percent x expected annual bonus payment). To compute the average contribution, we compute the mean value of the expected contribution of each member. All dollar figures are adjusted for inflation and placed in 1999 dollars.

To compute the average contribution under method 1, we require an estimate of reserve earnings. The 1992 reserve survey asked sample respondents about their total reserve earnings, before taxes and deductions, for all of 1991. The earnings figure included earnings from drills, annual training, bonuses, and pay from any call-ups or other active-duty service.

Clearly, this earnings figure includes some special and incentive pays. However, reserve earnings for 1991 are likely to be unduly large because of Operation Desert Storm and the large and relatively long call-up of part-time reservists. On the other hand, reservists today are often called to participate in peace-time operations. Still, reserve earnings today are likely to be less than the 1991 figure, adjusting for inflation. Thus, the estimate we use is likely to produce an overestimate of the average contribution to the TSP.

Because the TSP Board used average basic pay in its computation of the average contribution, its figure is considerably less than our estimate. Its estimate of average basic pay is $4892, while our earnings estimate from the 1992 survey is $7711.

Using Method 1, the Average Contribution Is Small, Though Larger than the TSP Estimate

	Method 1	TSP Board
Average annual earnings (1999 $)	$7,711*	$4,892**
Annual contribution rate	4.2%	4.2%
Expected annual contribution	$324	$205

* Includes earnings from drills, annual training/ACDUTRA, affiliation bonuses, and any call-ups or other active duty or active duty for training

**Average basic pay computed by TSP Board

A 1251 11/98   RAND

Yet, even using the higher $7711 figure and applying the 4.2 percent contribution rate, the estimated average annual reserve contribution is only $324. Although larger than the $200 figure roughly estimated by the TSP Board, this figure is small.

Method 2 produces a larger estimate of the average annual part-time reserve TSP contribution. Average basic pay among the 1992 reserve survey respondents, adjusted to 1999 dollars, was $5351, a figure that is somewhat higher than the TSP Board's estimate. Like the board, we assume that reservists would contribute 4.2 percent of basic pay to the TSP. As discussed earlier, we assume that the 18 percent of enlisted reservists who receive bonuses would contribute the full amount (100 percent) to the TSP, and we assume that the annual bonus payment for all reservists who get one to be $2500. We compute the expected contribution for each reserve survey sample respondent and take the mean. We find that the average expected annual contribution is $532, a figure that far exceeds the $200 figure that the TSP Board estimates or the $324 we estimate under Method 1.

Nonetheless, the $532 figure is still relatively small compared with what a low-grade GS federal civil service employee would contribute annually. We make a rough estimate and find that the average contribution of a GS 1–5 civil service employee is $918, almost double the figure we estimate for the reserve participants.

To arrive at the $918 estimate, we use available information (the 1996 TSP Board Demographics Report) that indicates that about 25 percent of individuals who earn about $23,000 do not contribute to the TSP and only receive the automatic 1 percent government match that the Federal Employees Retirement System provides for employees hired after 1983.

We assume that the 75 percent who do contribute are contributing 5 percent of their pay. Using information on the number of workers in each grade from the Office of Personnel Management, using the FY99 federal civil service GS pay table, and assuming that individuals are at step 5 in their grade, we estimate the average pay of GS 1–5 workers to be about $23,000. Putting these figures together, we estimate an annual contribution of $918.

To summarize our main findings, we estimate that the number of part-time reserve accounts will be large, equal to 54,800, but fewer than the number of accounts estimated by the TSP Board.

As noted earlier, it is possible that we underestimate the participation rate because we base the rate on an estimate of participation in an IRA, and contributions to an IRA may be treated differently for tax purposes than contributions to the TSP. We conducted a sensitivity analysis and found that even if 30 percent, rather than 20 percent, participated in a nonmatching fund, the estimated reserve TSP participation rate would be at most 12 percent, and therefore still less than what the TSP Board estimates. Therefore, our overall conclusions are not affected by this potential problem.

We attempted to account for the reservists' being able to contribute their special and incentive pays to their TSP accounts, and therefore being likely to have larger account balances than what the board estimates. We used two alternative methods to estimate the average expected reserve contribution amount from those who participate and found the average to be $324 under the first method and $532 under the second. Both figures are considerably larger than the roughly $200 average that the board estimates. Nonetheless, these averages are still quite small, even when compared to low-grade personnel in the civil service for whom we estimate an average expected contribution of about $900.

Of course, if prior-service reservists could contribute to the accounts that they created while active-duty personnel, the number of accounts would be even fewer. Estimating how few was beyond the scope of our analysis. Alternatively, if prior-service reservists could roll over their active account balance to a reserve TSP account, the number of reserve accounts would not be fewer, but the average balance would be even larger than what we estimate here. Again, determining how much larger was beyond the scope of our study.

Reserve Participation Will Only Increase the Total Number of TSP Accounts by 2.5%

TSP Participation Among:		Percentage increase due to reserve participation
Federal civil service	2,000,000*	
Active-duty personnel	148,000**	
Reserve personnel	54,800	
Total	2,202,800	2.5%

* Source: 1996 TSP demographics report, TSP Board
**Estimated as 10% participation rate x 1,480,000 active-duty personnel

A 1251 11/98   RAND

While 54,800 is a substantial number of accounts, it is only a small fraction of the number of accounts that the TSP manages overall.

According to the 1996 TSP Demographics Report, there are about 2 million federal civil service TSP accounts. If, as a rough estimate, we assume that 10 percent of the 1,480,000 active-duty personnel would participate in the TSP, the total number of accounts would be about 2,202,800. The 54,800 accounts associated with part-time reserve participation are only 2.5 percent of this total. The participation rate for active-duty personnel may be even lower than 10 percent, given their relatively young ages. However, even if fewer active-duty personnel participated, the fraction of total accounts that were due to reserve participation would still be less than 5 percent of the total.

The TSP Board contends that the cost of administering the reserve accounts could not be spread over all of the accounts that it manages, which would include the civil service accounts. However, if there are economies of scale associated with managing a large number of accounts, the additional cost at the margin—that is, the marginal cost rather than the average cost—of managing reserve accounts might be relatively small.

The policy options we suggest focus on ways to increase the average part-time reserve contribution and on ways to reduce the number of part-time reserve account holders.

An obvious approach to increasing account contributions among part-time reservists is simply to allow them to contribute more of their basic pay to their TSP accounts. One way to do this is to eliminate the 5-percent ceiling. However, because they only work part-time in their military jobs, reservists do not, on average, earn much basic pay annually. The low annual pay levels limit the potential for large account balances being produced by eliminating the 5-percent ceiling. Another way to increase reserve account balances is to mandate a minimum contribution or account balance for all personnel. Establishing a minimum annual contribution of, say, $1000 would reduce the number of accounts as well as increase their average size.

Because many reservists are prior-service personnel and many are federal employees, it is possible that a single individual could maintain more than one TSP account. As shown earlier, the reserve survey indicates that 16 percent of respondents worked for the federal government. A large number of reservists are prior service. Theoretically, some individuals could maintain as many as three accounts: one for their active duty, one for their federal civil service, and one for the reserve duty. Clearly, if individuals were allowed to consolidate their TSP accounts, the overall number of TSP accounts is likely to be fewer. The feasibility of allowing individuals to consolidate accounts should be investigated further.

Finally, insofar as adding part-time reservists to the TSP system would place an additional burden on the TSP Board's computer system, additional funding should be provided to the board to upgrade its systems to handle these accounts.

APPENDIX: CPS PROBIT RESULTS FOR PROBABILITIES OF HAVING A DC PLAN AND AN IRA

This appendix contains probit equations for the probability of having a defined contribution plan and the probability of participating in a non-employer matched savings plan. They were estimated using data from the Benefits Supplement of the April 1993 Current Population Survey. The advantage of this dataset is that it can be used to estimate how these probabilities vary with personal characteristics such as age, race, sex, and income, which cannot be done with data based on employer surveys. The Benefits Supplement was administered to a subset of the individuals in the April 1993 CPS (about 23,000 valid responses). In addition to responses to the Benefits Supplement, the data contain the individual-level information based on the basic CPS for April 1993 and the March 1993 Annual Demographic Survey (ADS). The latter contains retrospective questions about each individual's activities and earnings during 1992. We extracted the subset of individuals in the Benefits Supplement who (1) were 20+ years old, (2) gave a valid response to the question of "how many employees are employed by your employer" (based on the March 1993 ADS), (3) were employed at the time of the April 1993 survey, and (4) had some earnings in 1992. The sample contained 18,024 individuals meeting these criteria.

54.3 percent of those in our sample worked for an organization providing a retirement plan for at least some employees. 88.8 percent of those working for a firm with a retirement plan said that they were eligible to participate in the plan. Only 20 percent were participating in a defined contribution plan (about 41 percent of those eligible to participate in an employer-provided plan). This participation rate is lower than the participation rates reported in the BLS Establishment Surveys.

We believe there are three reasons for this difference. First, the Establishment Surveys are more recent and participation in defined contribution plans has been on the rise in the 1990s. Second, employers may be in a better position than employees themselves to report the kind of retirement plan in which employees are participating (many individuals might not understand the distinction between defined contribution and defined benefit systems). Third, the CPS does not actually survey individuals, but household heads, and household heads might not be fully informed about other household members' participation in retirement systems or the type of plan in which they are participating.

We handled the apparent underreporting of participation in a defined contribution plan by weighting the observations in the probit model for DC plan participation so that the model produced a mean participation rate of 39 percent (so weighted because BLS Establishment data indicates that 39 percent is roughly the economy-wide participation in DC plans among those employed).

Data on the likelihood of participating in a nonemployer matched savings plan are not readily available. The TSB used the participation of CSRS employees in FERS TSP as a proxy for participation in a nonmatched plan (overall 20 percent; adjusted downward to 16 percent to account for the lower earnings of reservists). We used the CPS respondents' participation in an IRA as a proxy for participation in a nonmatched IRA. 20.5 percent of respondents said they had an IRA. This rate is close to the rate assumed by the TSP and is also close to data from tax returns reported by the IRS.

Probit models are models for discrete events and are based on the cumulative normal distribution. Letting P represent the probability of an event (e.g., participation in a DC plan), X represent a set of variables, and b represent a coefficient vector, the probability of an event is $P = F(Xb)$, where F denotes the cumulative normal distribution evaluated at Xb. Let DP represent the change in the probability of the event due to a change in one of the variables in X. It may be shown that $DP = bf$ where f is a factor that converts the coefficients to probability changes.

Results are displayed in Table 1. The first column for each model shows the probit coefficients (the b's). The second column shows the t-statistics associated with the coefficients. The third column shows the significance level associated with each estimate. The fourth column shows the effect of a change in each variable on the relevant probability. It should be emphasized that these coefficient estimates and probability changes show the effects of the variable in question, holding other factors constant. Although the two probit equations were estimated with the same data, the sample sizes differ because of differences in the number of missing values of the dependent variable across equations.

To interpret the results, consider the effect of working for an organization with more than 100 employees (Large Org). The coefficient (0.467) has a t-statistic of 18.08 and is significant at the 0.0001 level, meaning that there is only one chance in ten thousand that the effect of firm size actually has no effect on the probability of having a DC plan. The probability change of 0.180 says that individuals working in an organization with more than 100 employees are 18 percentage points more likely to have a DC plan than individuals working for an organization with fewer than 100 employees. Similarly, full-time workers are significantly more likely to have a DC plan than part-time workers (with a probability difference of 0.106). Interestingly, employees of large organizations and full-time workers are less likely to have an IRA than employees of small organizations or part-time workers, probably because these workers are more likely to have employer-provided retirement plans.

The probability of having a DC plan or an IRA generally rises with income and age, although the effects are not linear (see table). Males are less likely than females to have either a DC plan or an IRA. Racial differences also exist, with whites more likely, and blacks less likely, to have either a DC plan or an IRA than individuals of all other races.

Table 2 provides the average values of the variables in the probit models and the average values of the same variables from the 1992 Reserve Survey.

Table 1

Variable	Equation 1: Have DC Plan? (1 = Yes; 0 = No)				Equation 2: Have IRA? (1 = Yes; 0 = No)			
	Estimate	T-Stat	Sign.	ΔP	Estimate	T-Stat	Sign.	ΔP
Intercept	−2.707	25.42	0.0010		−1.740	16.09	0.0010	
Income range in $1000 (omitted = less than $10,000):								
10–19	0.435	9.63	0.0001	0.167	0.205	4.57	0.0001	0.071
20–29	0.612	12.92	0.0001	0.235	0.554	11.87	0.0001	0.193
30–39	0.806	15.91	0.0001	0.310	0.749	14.85	0.0001	0.260
40–49	0.829	14.65	0.0001	0.319	0.993	17.69	0.0001	0.345
50–59	0.974	14.61	0.0001	0.375	1.044	15.69	0.0001	0.363
60–69	1.075	12.99	0.0001	0.413	1.313	16.07	0.0001	0.457
70–79	0.881	8.40	0.0001	0.339	1.279	12.55	0.0001	0.445
80–89	1.203	9.91	0.0001	0.463	1.445	12.09	0.0001	0.502
90–99	1.175	12.14	0.0001	0.452	1.545	16.22	0.0001	0.537
100+	1.051	5.02	0.0001	0.404	1.827	8.46	0.0001	0.635
Age range (omitted = less than age 25):								
25–29	0.164	2.92	0.0036	0.063	0.232	3.03	0.0025	0.080
30–34	0.283	5.11	0.0001	0.109	0.524	7.12	0.0001	0.182
35–39	0.291	5.19	0.0001	0.112	0.702	9.56	0.0001	0.244
40–44	0.214	3.70	0.0002	0.082	0.788	10.58	0.0001	0.274
45–49	0.215	3.64	0.0003	0.083	0.970	12.93	0.0001	0.337
50–54	0.269	4.37	0.0001	0.104	1.156	15.12	0.0001	0.402
55–59	0.232	3.62	0.0003	0.089	1.290	16.58	0.0001	0.449
Class of worker:								
Private	1.122	17.45	0.0001	0.432	−0.416	8.74	0.0001	−0.145
Federal	0.453	5.49	0.0001	0.174	−0.543	7.23	0.0001	−0.189
State & local	0.428	6.13	0.0001	0.164	−0.407	7.25	0.0001	−0.142
Work characteristics:								
Work full-time	0.275	7.75	0.0001	0.106	−0.141	3.99	0.0001	−0.049
Large org	0.467	18.08	0.0001	0.180	−0.086	3.27	0.0011	−0.030
Demographic characteristics:								
Male	−0.087	3.63	0.0003	−0.033	−0.185	7.22	0.001	−0.064
White	0.149	2.55	0.0108	0.057	0.110	1.80	0.0718	0.038
Black	−0.054	0.76	0.4449	−0.021	−0.491	5.95	0.0001	−0.171
Married	0.072	2.22	0.0264	0.028	0.224	6.47	0.0001	0.078
Single	0.015	0.35	0.7259	0.006	0.262	5.65	0.0001	0.091
Sample size	18024				17790			
Dep var mean	0.39				0.205			
Log-likelihood	−9004.1				−7736.7			

Table 2

	CPS		Reserve Survey	
	Mean	Std. Dev.	Mean	Std. Dev.
Income range in $1,000 (omitted = less than $10,000):				
10–19	0.267	0.443	0.158	0.364
20–29	0.234	0.424	0.213	0.409
30–39	0.151	0.358	0.176	0.381
40–49	0.080	0.272	0.101	0.301
50–59	0.039	0.193	0.056	0.229
60–69	0.019	0.138	0.026	0.158
70–79	0.011	0.104	0.014	0.119
80–89	0.007	0.086	0.008	0.088
90–99	0.014	0.116	0.003	0.053
100+	0.002	0.048	0.021	0.143
Age range (omitted = less than age 25):				
25–29	0.138	0.345	0.137	0.344
30–34	0.167	0.373	0.160	0.367
35–39	0.169	0.374	0.167	0.373
40–44	0.149	0.356	0.185	0.388
45–49	0.129	0.335	0.158	0.365
50–54	0.093	0.291	0.069	0.254
55–59	0.076	0.265	0.031	0.174
Class of worker:				
Private	0.756	0.430	0.504	0.500
Federal	0.039	0.192	0.254	0.435
State & local	0.150	0.357	0.180	0.384
Work characteristics:				
Work full-time	0.7763	0.4167	0.688	0.463
Large org	0.6323	0.4822	0.357	0.479
Demographic characteristics:				
Male	0.535	0.499	0.786	0.410
White	0.885	0.319	0.816	0.388
Black	0.076	0.266	0.107	0.309
Married	0.668	0.471	0.666	0.472
Single	0.187	0.390	0.197	0.398

BIBLIOGRAPHY

Bureau of Labor Statistics, "Employee Benefits in State and Local Governments, 1994," United States Department of Labor, USDL 95-368, Washington, D.C., 1995.

Bureau of Labor Statistics, "Employee Benefits in Medium and Large Private Establishments, 1997," United States Department of Labor, USDL-99-02, Washington, D.C., 1999.

Bureau of Labor Statistics, "Employee Benefits in Small Private Establishments, 1996," United States Department of Labor, USDL-98-240, Washington, D.C., 1998.

Bureau of the Census, Current Population Survey, April 1993, Survey of Employee Benefits, Technical Documentation, Washington, D.C., 1994.

Employee Benefits Research Institute, "EBRI Notes," Vol. 20, Number 12, December 1999.

Federal Retirement Thrift Investment Board, letter from Roger Mehle, Executive Director, to William Cohen, Secretary of Defense, December 22, 1999.

Federal Retirement Thrift Investment Board, letter from Roger Mehle, Executive Director, to Rudy deLeon, Under Secretary of Defense for Personnel and Readiness, August 26, 1999.

Federal Retirement Thrift Investment Board, *Analysis of 1996 Thrift Savings Plan Participant Demographics*, 1997.

Kirby, Sheila Nataraj, David Grissmer, Stephanie Williamson, and Scott Naftel, *Cost and Benefits of Reserve Participation, New Evidence from the Reserve Components Survey*, Santa Monica, Calif. RAND, MR-812-OSD, 1997.

Uniform Services Almanac Inc., *Reserve Forces Almanac 2000*, Falls Church, VA.